The FIZBO Manual

Successfully Selling Your Home Yourself
is Now Possible

Learn How to Sell Your Home Yourself in A Stress-Free Manner

Thomas (TJ) Underwood

The FIZBO Manual

Library of Congress Cataloging-in-Publication Data

Copyright© 2021, 2023 by Thomas (TJ) Underwood

The FIZBO Manual: A concise and to the point guide on how you can successfully sell your home yourself in any economic environment and achieve the goals that you desire most in a more efficient and effective manner.

Printed in the United States of America

Self-Published

Text design by Thomas (TJ) Underwood

ISBN: 978-1-953994-10-3

INTRODUCTION

Wow, God works in unpredictable ways as I was working on 3 to 4 other books that I was in the process of completing when the inspiration to create **The FIZBO Manual** occurred.

However, with the inspiration and thoughts occurring in a "rapid fire" manner I had no choice but to respond to the inspiration and put **The FIZBO Manual** on the market at this time.

Hopefully that burst of inspiration will help those who are now considering selling their home themselves a real guide that will take them toward the success that they desire.

As much as I rail against procrastination, I realized that the power of procrastination had gripped me for several months—to a degree.

No excuses have been my mantra—and it should be yours as well! Even though I have really been extremely busy this year and have been pulled in what seems like a million different directions, my focus and commitment to assist consumers worldwide in the management and improvement of their credit and finances have remained steadfast.

We all must at this time reach higher—and achieve more!

The FIZBO Manual (updated in 2023) is designed to give those who desire to sell their home themselves the realistic actions that they will need to take to get their home sold in a timely manner and at a fair price.

Everything that a **For Sale By Owner** seller needs to know if they sincerely desire to get results that will show can be found in this short and to-the-point guide!

Why abandon your dreams now when you could at this time decide to do something great for yourself and your family. Will you pursue financial gain, or will you continue to complain?

Your success begins here…

How can you achieve what you need to achieve if you don't move your feet? Sit—Stand—Walk—

Run—Backflip and do what is necessary to make your dreams happen.

When God says it is time to happen it will happen—however it is up to you to act on a consistent basis to put in motion what is needed to make it happen!

Isn't it time that you make something big happen in your life. It starts in a major way by successfully selling your home.

The FIZBO Manual

Determining whether to sell your home as a **For Sale By Owner** is a BIG decision—but it no longer has to be a difficult one.

If you are contemplating selling your home yourself in the current market, there are some key questions that you must ask and answer appropriately to determine if you are a good candidate for selling your home yourself.

Those key questions that you must ask yourself among others include:

Am I in a position where I feel forced to sell my home?

What do I expect to gain by selling my home myself as opposed to hiring an agent?

Are homes selling in my neighborhood and/or surrounding area in a timely manner?

Is my home located in a highly desirable area?

Are there excellent schools in my neighborhood and school district?

Do I have the time that is needed and am I committed to showing, promoting, and doing all that is necessary including the research and other details that are required up to and after closing?

Are there any other special circumstances or details about my property or neighborhood such as environmental or other issues that negatively affect the property and/or area?

Do I know what I "need to net" and what I "want to net" from the sale of my home?

If you answered the above questions appropriately you may be a good candidate for selling your home yourself as a **FIZBO** or **F**or **S**ale **B**y **O**wner!

However, it is important that you are equipped with the right knowledge if you desire to sell your home the right way and with the least inconvenience and aggravation as possible.

The FIZBO Manual is designed to provide you with the pressing details that you need to know to increase the odds that you will sell your home in a timely manner and at a fair price for both you and the home buyer.

CONTENTS

Introduction

Chapter 1 An Overview of the For Sale By Owner (**FIZBO**) Process

Chapter 2 Curb Appeal & Preparing Your Home for the Current Market

Chapter 3 How To Price Your Home Appropriately In Today's Market

Chapter 4 How To Skillfully Negotiate The Closing

Chapter 5 The Complete Home Buying/Selling Process

Appendix A Thomas (TJ) Underwood—*Real Estate Broker, Financial Planner, Author, Blogger*

Appendix B Thomas (TJ) Underwood/TFA Financial Planning

Bonus Section: GOAL SETTING & MONEY MANAGEMENT PERSONALITIES

The FIZBO Manual

Copyright© 2021, 2023 by Thomas (TJ) Underwood

What others have said about The FIZBO Manual

"One of the most powerful books on the market—bar none—that is designed for those who desire to sell their home themselves."

"The FIZBO Manual will provide you a new and clearer way of looking at and completing the duties that you need to complete to make your home sale more prosperous and productive and helps you eliminate steps that you might make that would put you on the wrong path."

"The FIZBO Manual gives you the needed focus to help ensure that you don't miss a crucial step and lose out on a successful sale that serves your best interest."

The FIZBO Manual consists of 5 chapters and a Bonus Section.

This manual is designed to do more for you than just showing you the process in a highly effective way. **The FIZBO Manual** is also designed to inspire you to do what needs to be done in a timely manner so that you can reach your desired goals.

It is one thing to know what needs to be done to sell your home yourself. You must also put into action what you know if you are to get results that will show. Many consumers put their home on the market and try to sell it themselves without having the right knowledge—let alone acting on the right knowledge for their greater benefit.

If you now think that you can sell your home yourself, you can in many cases do so. However, will it be sold at the right price and in a timely manner? Will the proceeds net you what you need to net to pay off your mortgage and do what you like to do in your future?

Even if you don't have a mortgage on your property, you still want to sell your property in a manner that will benefit you and your family the most.

The FIZBO Manual is designed to meet those, and other concerns head on by giving you the knowledge that you need to act on. **The FIZBO Manual** will inspire you to do what needs to be done in a manner that serves you and your family the most, not creditors and others who may not have any real concern for your future success.

Many consumers know what they need to do to achieve success, but they fail to act on that knowledge because they don't have an effective system of providing them the blueprint of what to act on at any given time. They often drift from completing one task and drifting off and not completing the other tasks that need to be completed in a timely manner for them to reach their goal(s).

In short many know what to do, however very few actually do what they need to do! Which one are you?

Are you ready to take the right action on what you will soon know—so that you can obtain positive results that will show? **The FIZBO Manual** is designed to help you sell your home in a more effective manner so that you can pursue—your other goals and dreams—and make them come true!

Chapter 1

An Overview of the For Sale By Owner (FIZBO) Process

FSBO stands for **For Sale By O**wner and is also known by those in the real estate and finance industry as a **FIZBO**. Throughout this book you will see the acronym **FIZBO** and at all times you must realize that it refers to a person who is selling their home as a **For Sale By O**wner seller! Always realize that **FSBO** and **FIZBO** are one and the same and they are both pronounced as **fizz bow**.

The primary reason that many homeowners attempt to sell their home themselves is that they believe that they can sell their home at a better price and keep the commission (6 to 7 percent in many markets) that would normally go to the real estate agents. In many cases this assumption does not play out in the vast majority of cases as many homeowners often end up listing their home with an agent in the end.

They do so because they did not look out into the horizon and gather the right information to determine if their home was a good candidate for selling as a **FIZBO.**

Even though real estate agents have the benefit of the **Multiple Listing Service** (MLS) and other empowering marketing tools—that does not mean that you can't sell your home yourself at a fair price and in a timely manner.

You must assess your property condition, location and "recent sales environment" as well as determining proactively if you have the appropriate amount of time and you are willing to put forth the required effort that is needed to ensure a successful closing.

Since you purchased this book there is a strong likelihood that you (or a loved one) are **considering selling your home yourself.** Not all home sales require the assistance of a real estate agent (although they can be invaluable in many cases).

Do you have the time that is needed to market your property whether online, using yard signs and other print media—and have you researched your market area and determined what homes that are in the same condition as your home are selling for in your area and in what time frame are they sold in?

The FIZBO Manual is designed to help you enhance what you need to do to successfully sell your home yourself.

You can sell your home yourself—however **knowing the steps that are needed ahead of time** puts you well ahead of most consumers who are considering selling their home themselves—or those who are currently in the process of selling their home themselves, and even those who are considering listing with an agent.

Selling your home, yourself, requires far more than getting a **For Sale By Owner** sign and putting your name and number on it.

You need to know all the steps that are required prior to referring your buyer to your attorney.

Once you have a buyer. you want to contact a real estate attorney and they would help prepare the contract between the buyer and the seller (you) and take care of the closing.

Be advised that you normally must pay a fee for their services prior to the closing and also pay a fee for the actual closing.

In most states the seller normally pays for the title insurance and the documentary stamps on the deed. Many other closing costs are negotiable between the buyer and seller (you).

Will you be offering seller financing with your property? If so, you definitely need an attorney up front to help you draw up the contract and terms (prepare the note and mortgage or holding the financing).

If you desire to sell your home and you and you know a real estate agent and you are considering selling your home yourself, you may want to pay them to get timely market information.

Real estate agents can provide neighborhood information along with current market conditions based on your property condition and also help you determine if cosmetic repairs or upgrades need to be done prior to putting your home on the market.

Once you have a serious prospect your next step is to contact a real estate attorney—if you have not done so prior to putting your property on the market.

Many FIZBO's see the home flipping shows that are now popular on TV and think they can sell their house themselves and make a "profit."

They often think that the house will "sell itself." That might be the case in some instances, however—**you must know the likelihood on the front end** by doing the **necessary research in your market—not learn the hard way after your property lingers on the market for months.**

As a homeowner who is selling your home yourself, it is important that you do a great job in getting your home ready for viewing.

That might mean getting help from experts to get your house ready to sell, which typically involves changing the way the interior has looked (staging) by de-cluttering and re-arranging furniture.

When selling your home yourself, you must not be reluctant to change the appearance—as by making the necessary changes it can often help your home sell faster and at top dollar.

It can be hard to convince someone who has been living in their home for years (whether a **FIZBO** or a seller listing their property with an agent) that their taste in furniture, appliances, landscaping, or anything else is what is preventing the sale of their house—or is likely to prevent the sale in a timely manner at a better price.

However, that is exactly what **The FIZBO Manual** is trying to do—convince you up front that you must **prepare your property (and mind) optimally** for a successful sale by **doing the needed market research up front** and preparing your property for the current market by making sure it is in **"selling condition."**

Many home buyers are turned off by homeowners who have an odd or unusual approach to furniture, interior painting, unusual carpet colors and the like. I have seen firsthand the negative reaction of potential buyers in all too many instances due to homeowners not doing what is required—on the front end.

Your Attitude and Outlook Is Critical for a Successful Sale

After you have done your market research and prepared the property for the current market and you have your FSBO sign up along with all your other marketing methods in place, your next step is to wait until a buyer comes with an offer that is acceptable to you.

Creating **FSBO signs** are very simple as all there is to it is a "For Sale By Owner" and a phone number on the sign. Make sure it is as professional as possible by using a print shop or office supply store.

Once you have a serious prospect, your next step is to contact a real estate attorney if you have not done so prior to putting your property on the market.

Why Pricing Is Critical Whether FIZBO or Listing with An Agent

In the wake of the "boom" of the early 2000's where homeowners and agents got away with overpricing, a homeowner is now more likely to get a low-ball offer on a grossly inflated asking price. The seller then becomes impatient, then panicky and they often cave in greatly on their price when a loss of sale appears imminent.

Many **FIZBO** homeowners who attempt to sell their home themselves often look at their homes as liquid assets and **expect way too much profit when they sell.**

The market is always changing, and you want to know if you are in a buyers, sellers, or transitioning market. Many markets have corrected and are now getting back to what it should be--and single-family homes prices are getting back to where they should be since the major housing market decline from 2007 to 2009 occurred.

As of August 2023, many markets have homes that have appreciated significantly making home ownership qualification difficult for many potential buyers. In many markets affordable inventory of homes are at an all-time low.

How many **FIZBO's** do you think are savvy with their sales and marketing?

Very Few!

If you show that you are savvy as a **FIZBO** by pricing your home right, marketing your property appropriately and doing the necessary research upfront, you have completed an important process and successfully selling your home at market price is now made more realistic for you and your family!

Why Timing is Important Whether FIZBO or Listing with An Agent

In the wake of the "boom times," homeowners think it is easy to sell a house. It often can be however you must still do your research upfront and market your home in a savvy manner to get the right offers.

You don't want to be one of those **FIZBO's** who price their home at an inflated price, thinking they can sell at an inflated price and pocket the money that they would have given as commission to a real estate agent—or lower the price later after months on the market with no offers.

On the surface, selling your home yourself seems great, but many **FIZBO's** who overprice their home found their homes on the market for extended periods of time, bringing the value down and forcing them to reduce their selling price—often substantially—**when with the proper research on the front end**, it probably would not have been necessary.

When the market is slow, and homes are not selling as fast it can often be difficult for a **FIZBO** or any home seller to sell their property in a timely manner and at a fair price. Because buyers know the market is slow, they will often submit lowball offers—even more often when dealing with **a FIZBO**.

As mentioned earlier in this chapter, many **FIZBO's** see the home flipping shows and real estate shows on TV and think that they can sell their home themselves and make a "profit." However, the process is not as easy as they make it look as in most cases it will take effort on your part to consummate a successful sale!

Your willingness to approach the hard truths, in a real way, is what will set you apart from your **FIZBO** competition--and even your competition of homes in your area that are listed by an agent.

Where a **FIZBO** who has not done the **proper research on the front end** will cave in on price before they necessarily must, a smart **FIZBO** seller like you will know the sales price range of your home based on the current condition of your home and the current market conditions (what homes are currently selling for).

In short, you know that your home is **FIZBO sell-ready (you have done the necessary research prior to putting your home on the market)**.

It's no wonder that those who try to sell their home themselves often become frustrated—they have not done their research properly on the FRONT end!

In **Chapter 2** we will dive into what you specifically need to do to ensure a successful outcome in the selling of your home by preparing your home for the current market

Chapter 2

Curb Appeal & Preparing Your Home for the Current Market

As the **Home Buying Season** rapidly approaches (generally May through September in many markets) many home sellers are contemplating putting their home on the market and move to another location.

Over the years we have seen many homeowners **successfully sell their home** and there are certain areas of understanding **(particularly curb appeal)** that are very important to a successful sale.

Curb Appeal—or how your home looks upon arrival is a critical component of **selling your home** yourself and it will be discussed in a manner that can help you sell your home in a timelier manner and at a better market price.

It is important that you improve the **"curb appeal"** of your home **prior to** putting your home up for sale if you desire to maximize your sales proceed and move to an area that you desire. Even if you don't plan on moving, improving the curb appeal of your home could be a worthwhile effort as it can provide you a more relaxing and entertaining environment that you can enjoy daily in your current environment.

It is important that you realize that the **exterior of your home** determines if many potential home buyers will even want to enter your home, therefore it is important that **your exterior is in the best position possible** because potential buyers form an opinion of the value of your home based on the exterior. If the exterior is not up to par in a buyer's mind—they will feel that the inside has been neglected even if it appears that there has been no neglect.

The **curb appeal** of your home is the first impression that a home buyer gets, and it is important that the first impression is a positive one. Many real estate agents often preview a home prior to showing the home and in some cases just a drive by is done—because they realize that if the **curb appeal** does not meet the standards of their buyer, their buyer(s) won't even enter the house.

A **poor curb appeal** will also cause **home appraisers** to lower their value of the appraisal and if your home **does not appraise at the selling**

price you may have to lower the price or renegotiate in some other manner.

If you are selling your home as a **FIZBO** most potential buyers will ride by and determine from the exterior look of your home if they want to see the inside.

Having said all of that—there are things that you can do prior to putting your home on the market that can **dramatically improve the curb appeal** of your home and get it sold faster and at top dollar.

You can do a combination of the following and start on a path to improving your finances significantly because of the sale:

- Improve Your Landscaping

- Clean Exterior of Home, Driveways, Walkways, Patios, Decks & Other Structures

- Update By Painting

Improve Your Landscaping

Your **curb appeal** of your home is based upon the total picture that a home purchaser gets upon arrival to your home.

Is your lawn, shrubs, and other features of your home such as flower beds, rock gardens and other creations on your property an additional feature worth considering paying extra for?

Is your vegetation pruned and is your grass neatly manicured?

If I **look at your home from the street** are trees and shrubs that are obscuring an otherwise beautiful landscape present? Does vegetation and trees dwarf your home making it appear smaller? Are vegetation and trees located too close to the house and foundation? Are there tree stumps on the property that obscure the true beauty of the home?

It is important that you realize that because you see your home every day, you may not have an objective reality of how your home exists in the eyes of potential home purchasers! Your siding, garage doors, windows, shutters, and trimming—along with other areas—may need repairing or replacement. Are the eaves and gutters and other hard to reach areas of your home in good condition?

Clean Exterior of Home, Driveways, Walkways, Patios, Decks & Other Structures

It is important that you create a **favorable impression** that is caused by your **landscaping, painting and overall cleanliness of your property.** However, if your driveways, walkways, patios, decks, and other structures are not up to par--you will be working in vain! You must ensure that your sidewalks, driveways, walkways, patios, decks, and any other area of concern—are in top condition and will not have a **negative influence** on those who see those areas for the first time.

Pressure washing your sidings, bricks, driveways, walkways, patios, decks, and any other area of concern can help improve the "visuals" of your property significantly for a relatively low cost. You can create a more favorable impression in the mind of home buyers by **looking at your home from the street** and doing the necessary landscaping and cleaning in the areas that need to be cleaned.

Update by Painting

If after **pressure washing** your home you do not feel that it leads to a proper showing of your home, you can decide to paint your home—either partially or in full and add to the resale value of your home significantly.

Even if you do modest adjustments such as trim, door and shutters only—you can add tremendously to the resale value of your home.

If you need to re-visit your home exterior color scheme altogether—be sure to do so if it will aid in the resale value of your home.

Final Thoughts on Curb Appeal & Selling Your Home

It is important that you use common sense when **putting your home on the market for sale.** If the property does not appear to be in selling condition to you—it won't appear to be in selling condition to others—**however always**

realize that your opinion will more than likely be biased.

It is imperative that you make a **sincere effort** to get your property in **selling condition** and do what is necessary **to the best of your ability** to make **your home sale occur** in a manner that leads to you getting the best price and terms available based on the current market and condition of your property!

Don't overlook decks, fences, mailboxes, birdbaths, gazebos, and other decorative features on your property. Be sure to **thoroughly clean all areas on the exterior that need cleaning** and **repair any loose or broken items.** If necessary, you may need to paint or stain certain areas to help improve the overall beauty of your exterior.

Be sure your **front door area and the walkway that leads up to the doorway are in good repair** or replace if necessary. Keep in mind you may need to replace the hardware as well—such as mailboxes, house numbers, doorknobs and other areas that may seem small and insignificant to you but will mean a lot to those who are looking at your home for the first time.

You may also need to **refresh the exterior body and trim on your house** to make it stand out from other homes in the neighborhood or those currently on the market in the area that you live in. You can add to your **curb appeal** by creating interesting areas in your landscape. It doesn't have to get expensive as in many cases you can accent your home and landscape with planters or containers of various sizes, shapes, and colors to create a more visual environment than other homes that are currently on the market.

Keep in mind if you have properly maintained your home over the years, you will normally have to do less around **curb appeal** than those who have neglected their home. Regardless of where you now stand, utilizing the above **curb appeal tips** can help transform the look, feel and comfort of your home—inside and out and make it more desirable for home buyers in your market **or more enjoyable for you if you decide to stay put**.

It is important that you realize that **you now possess** much of what you need to know to get your property sold efficiently and at a **price that is acceptable** to you.

You can now make your dream of selling your home **at your price and terms** occur—and you now no longer must wonder if it is for sure.

By effectively utilizing the above **curb appeal** improvement tips you can improve the odds of selling your home at a price that is fair to you and the buyer more likely.

Now that you have an appreciation for getting your home ready for the market, let's talk about pricing your home appropriately so that your home does not stay on the market for an unnecessary amount of time. In Chapter 3 we will do just that!

Chapter 3

How to Price Your Home Appropriately in Today's Market

In this chapter you will find useful ideas and approaches that have worked for many past home sellers that can also **enhance the pricing of your home** and make your selling process easier as a **FIZBO** or as a traditional seller if you later decide to list your property with a real estate agent.

Overview of Home Pricing

It is important that you realize that the **final listing** (the price that you decide to sell with a real estate agent on the listing agreement) **and selling price** is your choice in the end.

However, if you decide to list too high—some real estate agents won't take your listing because they know that the price is unrealistic, and an over-priced listing will have a negative effect on their reputation/brand.

At the other extreme are agents who will take and list your property at almost any price because they don't fully understand the pricing and market dynamics that are at play!

You may decide to list for a price that gets your home sold in less time than **average days on the market**, or you may choose to list at a price that **may lead to fewer showings and more time on the market.**

As a **FIZBO,** you may have to pay a real estate agent to provide you current market data, however it is generally money well spent. Many agents may even do it as a complimentary service if you agree to list with them if you are unable to sell your property—or agree to purchase your next home by utilizing their services.

The following Items must be considered by you when setting a price for your home!

Condition:

The **condition of your home** affects the price and the speed of the sale. As home buyers often make purchases based on emotion—<u>first impressions are VERY important.</u> You must optimize the **"curb appeal"** (how your property looks upon arrival) of your property.

You must do so to optimize the physical appearance of your home in the home buyers mind *and maximize the home buyer's perception of the value of your home.*

A property that is inappropriately priced and in **poor condition compared to the competition** will often expire on the market (won't sell) and as a seller you would be disappointed as to why, when in many cases it was caused by an inappropriate mix of—condition compared to the competition—timing and location, right from the start.

It is important that you and/or your agent work to price your property appropriately from the outset based on the **condition versus the competition and current market conditions!**

Competition:

Those who are shopping for a home in certain price ranges are going to **compare your property against others** in the same or similar condition and price range.

Therefore, you must be aware of other listings in and around your neighborhood. This is where paying a real estate agent for market data comes in handy when you are trying to sell your home yourself.

Those **buyers will determine value** based on properties that they have already seen, properties that are currently listed or properties that have recently sold in the area.

Timing:

Property values are affected by the current real estate market. Are you in a buyer's market or a seller's market? Is the economy booming or is economic activity slow?

Is it peak buying time or is it a slow season?

Because you can't manipulate the market, you will have to formulate a pricing and marketing strategy that will take advantage of the **first 30 days** that your property is listed to be the most effective.

The **first 30 days** are when buyers and their agents discover your property and **the time when they are most likely to visit and make offers.**

Or another way of looking at it is—**the first 30 days offers you the best opportunity that you will have to sell your home!**

Location:

The single most important factor in determining the value of your property is **the area in which it is located.**

If you are in an area with strong schools, a diverse work force, strong government, solid infrastructure and close to amenities that consumers desire, you will generally be able to price your property higher than those whose property is in a less desirable area.

Therefore, when determining price, condition versus the competition, timing, **and location must be properly analyzed** to maximize your opportunity to sell during this **crucial 30-day window** or time frame!

Intangibles:

If the property that you are selling has features that are superior to other properties with a similar look in the same area such as a builder's home with better material, a home with a side entry garage and many other features—that could make a difference in the pricing.

A [clean, clutter free and neat looking home](#) will sell faster and at a better price than one that is in disarray and has a feel of having too much going on—within the walls and on the exterior.

The Pricing Basics Mentioned Above Are Just the Beginning When Selling Your Home

In the end when determining price, condition versus the competition, timing, and location must be properly analyzed to maximize your opportunity to sell in a shorter time frame than those who over-price their home right from the start!

When you put your home on the market with a real estate agent, they will normally compile comparative pricing of homes in your area, post a sign in your yard or place your home in the **MLS Listings**.

Most real estate agents will offer these services as a part of their overall services as they are standard throughout the industry and should be expected by you.

Listing your home with a highly competent real estate agent will usually produce better results than if you decided to sell on your own without the assistance of a real estate agent.

Pricing your home is a complex task and normally requires expertise. If your selling price is set too high, potential **buyers may be deterred from even considering your home** for viewing.

However, if you as a **FIZBO** do your research up front—you too can price your home successfully.

It is important that you **arrive at the optimal price** by evaluating and understanding the current market conditions, and the marketable features of your home. <u>And you may be able to do it yourself if you have the time and know how!</u>

It is important that you realize that the higher your home is priced above market value, the fewer the number of buyers that will be available to look at your property—generally speaking!

It is also important that you understand the **selling price of recently sold properties** with attributes like your property.

Your goal should be to arrive at a listing price that is attractive enough for buyers to request showings and make acceptable offers.

An active real estate agent who is tuned in to your market area can help you determine what properties are competing for the attention of buyers right now and determine what properties have not sold.

Unsold or expired properties are a good indicator of what prices buyers are unwilling to pay under current market conditions in your area.

Bringing Buyers to Your Home

Understanding where buyers come from allows real estate agents to market your home more effectively.

While buyers use a variety of information sources to learn about homes for sale in their target neighborhood and price range, **the vast majority** will discover your home with the assistance of a real estate agent in most markets.

Marketing Your Home

The more exposure your home receives, the more opportunity you'll have to sell at a fair price and in a timely manner.

In addition to internet and print media advertising, most real estate agents can attract qualified buyers by using the following methods:

- Property Flyer - prepare a professional marketing sales tool including graphics and highlights of your home to distribute to the brokerage community and potential buyers.

- MLS - Information about your home will be included in the MLS - a database of currently available properties accessible only by real estate agents

- Other Brokers - if you list with a real estate agent they can cooperate with and invite other brokers in the community to tour your home in order to find a buyer.

- Relocation Networks - Prospects for your home also come from relocation services, corporations, executive search firms and other real estate agents who keep track of potential buyers and maintain relationships with former clients.

- Referral Network - Sales meetings allow agents to present new listings to each other. Other real estate agents then refer to their client databases to identify potential buyers and arrange showing appointments.

As a FIZBO, you will have to do as much of the above as you see fit and are able to do. If your property does not sell in a timely manner you may have to come up with even better strategies to sell your home after potential buyers have viewed your home.

Chapter 4

How to Skillfully Negotiate the Closing

Skillful Negotiation

When offers are presented, **a skilled real estate agent** can advise you and help you obtain the best possible price and terms. However, as a FIZBO, it is **your duty** (along with **your real estate attorney**—you'll need to hire one) to come to agreement on the best price and terms.

Understanding the **various standard contract forms** and the vast array of **special stipulations and issues** that can arise is the **responsibility of your attorney.** Be sure you are aware of key negotiating terms, and you ultimately net the proceeds that are needed to meet your and your family's needs or future goals.

Making sure **buyers are qualified** is of the utmost importance in negotiating a successful sale in the current environment--whether a **FIZBO** or a traditional seller.

A skillful real estate attorney that you hire will promote **your interests as a home seller** and assist in **developing a clear and binding contract** that serves your best interest.

Managing the Transaction

There are a number of details that must be performed before a home sale becomes final, including inspections, repairs, finalizing loan documents, contingency removals, and insurance—to name a few.

You want to know how difficult and time consuming this process is upfront—not in the middle of the process! You want to know that the scheduling of inspections, reviewing documents, and making sure all the required disclosure forms and loan closing documents are provided in a timely fashion.

In essence you want to manage the closing effectively and efficiently!

If you desire a closing that is as stress free as possible for you and your family—it is imperative that **you choose a real estate attorney who can handle your home selling transaction in a**

highly skilled manner and relieve you of the burden of dealing with the more stressful areas of selling your home that will occur from contract to closing.

Be prepared to pay a reasonable fee for the service and realize long-term that the assistance of a skilled real estate attorney can be of great value and can save you a lot of effort and time—and help you reach your future goals in a timelier manner.

Final Conclusion

By **pricing your home appropriately** right from the start—you enhance the likelihood of a sale in a reasonable time at a **price that is favorable for the needs of both you and the home purchaser.**

As a For Sale By Owner seller you must realize that you will be competing against the following "Home Buying Options" that buyers have:

1) **Purchase directly from** (other For Sale By Owner home seller)—often called a resale

purchase—home is often listed with a real estate company or sold as a FSBO (For Sale By Owner)

2) New Purchase—purchase from a home builder, bank, or real estate office—a newly built property where buyer would be the first to live in

3) HUD Home—resale purchase where property was lost due to delinquency by previous owner and an FHA loan was involved

4) Fannie Mae—resale purchase where foreclosure occurred by previous owner and a Fannie Mae insured loan was involved

5) Freddie Mac—resale purchase where foreclosure occurred by previous owner and a Freddie Mac insured loan was involved

6) REO or Bank Owned—resale purchase where foreclosure occurred by previous owner and bank repossessed the property due to delinquency of previous owner and placed into bank inventory of homes--often called Real Estate Owned or Bank Owned

7) Short Sale—a sale in which home seller is in a difficult financial position and wishes to sell property for less than what is owed on the loan—requires lender and possibly other parties' approval—in addition to sellers' approval

8) Other—FDIC, and other government and non-governmental owned properties including auctioned properties and properties on the market by new entrants such as Zillow, Trulia, Open Door, Real Estate Brokerages, and others

Also keep in mind that the type of purchase that a buyer desires to make will influence the mortgage loan that buyer would select (or the one that serves buyer(s) best interest) unless buyer(s) was making a cash purchase.

You can learn more about all the above properties by navigating our websites that can be found at the end of this book.

As a FIZBO it is imperative that you do the needed research and price your home right—right from the start!

The FIZBO Manual has given you a new and fresh outlook on the home selling process and you are now equipped to sell your home yourself currently, if that is what you desire.

All of the key concerns that a **For Sale By Owner** seller needs to know if they sincerely desire to get results that will show has been provided to you in this short manual!

Why abandon your dreams now when you could at this time decide to do something great for yourself and your family by selling your home yourself.
In addition to effective negotiation, you want to be aware of the potential of exclusion from taxation ($250,000 single and $500,000 married filing joint) of the proceeds from the sale of your home if you meet the qualifications.

The **FIZBO Manual** has provided you an outlook on selling your home that is **doable by you** and can get you on a path to achieving your other goals or life ambitions.

To add even more clarity and to further reduce the stress level that could occur because of selling your home yourself, "the complete home buying/selling process" will be discussed in **Chapter 5** so that you are on sound footing as to what to potentially expect as you close on the successful selling of your home.

Chapter 5

The Complete Home Buying/Selling Process

In this chapter I will go over the complete home buying process to give you an overall assessment and better understanding of what you can expect during your closing process. Use the following as a guide only—as all home buying/selling processes are unique in nature.

What is the complete home buying/selling process?

Many potential home buyers and sellers have posed the above question—and it is a valid one—and one that they should pose prior to entering into a written contract for purchase whether you are a buyer or seller.

The Complete Home Buying/Selling Process:

It starts with preliminary home buyer pre-qualification to post-closing. As a for sale by owner seller--you want to ensure that the purchaser qualifies and has the means to purchase your home.

Therefore, ensuring that a buyer has a loan commitment from their lender, or the personal funds to close is a vital step.

Don't skip this step, many home sellers have skipped this step in the past to their own peril (failure to close on the selling of their home).

The home buying/selling process begins well before a buyer decides to place an offer on your home!

The preparation that you put into selling your home on the front end will pay great dividends on the back end if you do it the proper way.

If a buyer approaches you with an offer and they provide information from the lender stating that they are pre-approved as opposed to pre-qualified (more negotiating power) and the offer price is at or near your asking price—you want to give that offer serious consideration—generally.

In some instance the buyer may also have their own attorney or real estate agent upon presenting their offer, even while you sell your home as a for sale by owner seller!

After negotiation and a final sales price and terms are agreed to the buyer performs an inspection (usually a professional inspector is hired) based on the time limits specified in the offer that you agree to.

If there are problems of concern to the purchaser, you (and your attorney) counter the offer and negotiate until a final sales price is agreed to.

Once all contingencies are met the contract moves forward and the closing occurs.

Once the contract is accepted the buyer would make formal application for the loan (unless buying with cash) and once you receive the loan commitment letter (a contract between the purchaser and the lender) the process moves forward.

Once the inspection is complete and repairs are negotiated the contract continues to move forward. If no agreement is reached the contract may become null and void.

Assuming the contract moves forward and closing approaches after the buyer receives their mortgage commitment, the attorney(s) will submit a title insurance binder along with other legal paperwork required by buyer's lender.

Once everybody has signed off approval—a closing date can be set.

It is highly recommended that you allow the buyer to do a final walk through of your home that is under contract prior to closing.

The final walk through allows buyer(s) to reconfirm the condition of the house prior to closing. This normally happens a day or two before closing.

You want to allow this step because this is usually the buyer's last chance to verify that there has been no change or damage to the property, all agreed on repairs have been made, appliances that buyer expects to be there are still there and that your personal belongings have been removed if buyer will be moving in after closing—depending on negotiation.

Don't Assume Anything!

A lot can happen between accepting an offer and getting to the closing table.

Make sure that you bring photo identification to the closing. This is required since 9/11!

Real estate closings can often be exciting and stressful at the same time. There are many legal papers being shuffled back and forth, as well as checks for large sums of money being exchanged among parties.

At closing, you would give the title to the buyer in exchange for the purchase price that is stated in the contract. As a seller you would also deliver a deed, title evidence and a property survey if required.

The buyer brings insurance, termite letter, cashier's check etcetera.

You and or seller will be required to sign final mortgage papers, IRS Form 1099, a form formerly known as the HUD-1 statement or Uniform Settlement Statement and other Closing Documents.

The attorney will explain the purpose of each of these.

In addition, what the seller or buyer brings to closing—will vary depending on your locale, so be aware that state laws vary on buyer and seller responsibilities.

In addition, who brings what will vary based on how closing costs were negotiated.

In most cases, there are no warranties after closing. The only defects that you can make notice of or complain about are defects that you can prove were known and/or hidden defects that were not disclosed or could not have been found out about through a reasonable investigation.

After the sale, the deed and mortgage in buyers name will be registered and filed at the county recorder's office.

Be sure to save all your closing paperwork in a safe place.

You will need some of it for your taxes as you may have to report your gain even if the gain is excluded from taxation.

The closing documents are very important and due care should be utilized to safeguard them.

They are an inconvenience to replace and will cost you valuable time and money.

NOTE: The above home buying/selling process assumes 1st time buyer with no house to sell!

Also remember that all home buying and home selling situations are different and may require a more detailed offer and closing than that listed above.

Use the above home buying/selling process as a guide only—as each home buying/selling situation will be unique.

Once you successfully sell your home you may need to purchase another home or pursue other goals. In the next chapter **(BONUS CHAPTER)** we will look at goal setting and how you can use goal setting and effective money management to accomplish more in your future.

BONUS CHAPTER

Money Management Personalities

Today consumers are being pulled in many different directions when it comes to their credit and finances.

Mixed messages are often sent by many, so how do you decipher through all the noise to find information and advice that can truly move you and your family forward?

Whether <u>you perceive your current situation</u> to be caused by others, a lack of income, where you were born/raised or any other factor—it is important that you have a view (and you actually do so) of your future that includes **taking personal responsibility** (doing what you need to do and not waiting on others to do it for you)!

I basically state all of that to say that for the most part the "actions of others" are out of your control as you either can't do anything about it— or you won't do anything about it!

However, you can do a lot about <u>what you have under your control</u>—and <u>if you get your A I M</u>

right you can move forward in a more efficient and effective manner.

A—ttitude

I—ntellect

M—otivation

If you can get your **A I M right** (which you have absolute control over) you can pay off your outstanding consumer debt, retire in abundance, take that vacation that you always dreamed of— or attain any other goal or objective that you and your family may desire.

It is important that you cultivate an **A**ttitude that will lead to success on a consistent basis, and you use your brainpower (**I**ntelligence) appropriately and you stay **M**otivated at a high level!

Did you know that your Attitude—or the way that you think and feel about someone or something including how you look at and think about yourself and <u>your finances</u>—or a feeling or way of thinking that affects your behavior—or an expression of favor or disfavor toward a person, place, thing, or event—is a key factor in determining your future success in many facets of your life?

It is important that you realize that what holds most people back is that they blame others or make excuses <u>when they themselves actually have the power to transform their situation to that of success.</u>

You must realize that the right *Attitude* allows you to control your outcomes and not blame others! A mindset of <u>personal responsibility</u> provides you the <u>opportunity</u> to <u>manage distractions</u> and attain the future success that you desire—in all areas of your life!

If you do what you are <u>required to do</u> you can advance forward whether you did or did not cause your current situation! You <u>must have the mindset</u> that asks—**what can I do** to make my dreams come true? The right *Attitude* allows you to ask that question and answer it correctly and also puts your mind and thought process on a path to take <u>the right action!</u>

Did you know that how you use your Intelligence in terms of the many ways that you use:

<u>your logic</u>,

<u>abstract thought</u>,

<u>understanding</u>,

 <u>self awareness</u>,

<u>communication</u>,

<u>learning</u>,

<u>emotions</u>,

<u>memory</u>,

<u>planning</u>, and

<u>problem solving etcetera—is a key factor in determining your future success in many facets of your life?</u>

You possess inside <u>the knowledge</u> (or you will soon possess) of what you can do to make your dreams come true. By approaching your credit and finances in a more <u>intelligent manner</u> you increase the odds of success in your future!

By attacking your credit and finances *intelligently* you understand fully that it is your responsibility to do what you need to do to see your way through and you realize fully that it is never to your benefit to blame others or anything outside of yourself!

What are the future goals that I desire for myself and my family? What can I do to improve my **A I M**?

Did you know that the Motivation that lies within you is the driving force that causes you to **"move to action"** in a sincere manner and is a major determinant of your future success in all areas of your life?

Your Motivation for doing things causes you to optimize your well-being, minimize your physical pain—and maximize your pleasure.

Your *Motivation* can also originate from your specific physical needs such as eating, sleeping, resting, and other factors!

Motivation is an inner drive to behave or act in a certain manner. Your inner conditions such as your wishes, your desires, and **your goals**, activate you to move to action in a particular manner!

Your <u>motivation initiates, guides and maintains goal-oriented behaviors</u> that you now have or that you may have in the future.

Motivation is what causes you to act, whether it is getting a glass of water to reduce your thirst or reading and comprehending this book <u>to gain the knowledge that you need</u>—to succeed!

Motivation requires that you use the biological, emotional, social and cognitive forces within you that <u>activate behavior</u> that moves you toward what you desire.

In everyday usage, the term *motivation* is frequently used to describe *why* you would do something.

For example, you might say that you are *motivated* to <u>master the material in this book</u> so that you can live your life on your terms—not on the terms of creditors and others who have no real concern for your future. By doing so you can put yourself and your family in position to do what you really desire in your future!

As you **pursue your goals** you must never be <u>disappointed by your results</u> and <u>you must never stop too soon</u> as you can go further—you can push harder, your motivation must endure and you must ultimately expect success in your future!

Who says that you've done enough, accomplished enough? Why stop now?   You can go higher and higher—the "right movement" creates positive momentum—**consistent motivation and goal setting** helps propel that momentum!

What goals are you motivated towards accomplishing at this time?

You must never settle too quickly for too little! You must recognize success by the works that you provide and the success that you attain!

Did you know that people can see your worth by the works that you do, not what you proclaim (their eyes will be opened)?

A high level of motivation causes you to taste it and see it! Your actions and your movement toward your future goals must be so sincere that it provides all that and more!

You have many gifts, talents and abilities that may be lying dormant within you and now is the

time that you gain the knowledge of what you need to do!

You must realize that no one can make you read financial advice that is good for you—<u>but financial advice can be made available that can provide you with what you need to succeed</u> for you and others who are motivated toward achievement at a high level and those who <u>sincerely want to obtain empowering advice</u> that can lead to lasting success!

What is <u>inside of you</u> that you can use to make your dreams come true?

By having the <u>mindset that you will take personal responsibility</u> in all that you do—the power that is needed to transform your situation will be presented to you—if you do what you need to do!

It is important that <u>you use adversity that you may feel is happening to you for your and your family's future benefit</u> and you use *Motivation* to respond positively to that adversity!

It is also important to look at adversity from the vantage point that adversity is happening for you (your future benefit) as opposed to happening to you (why me)!

In this bonus chapter you have been presented powerful information that you can learn at a basic level and apply in your everyday life to help you attain a very high level of lasting success—
and <u>improve your A I M!</u>

Are you now just merely surviving (living for the now) or are you prospering (attaining success at a level that you can leave behind something for your heirs)?

Are you looking at **<u>new and more empowering ways of thinking and doing things</u>** or are you caught up in doing things in the <u>same manner as you did in the past</u> because it is more comfortable to you—<u>but not more comfortable for you?</u>

It is important that you realize that change <u>within your mind</u> must occur if you are to prosper (attain a higher level of success that provides you more than merely surviving) and achieve the type of success that you need to attain or the type of success that you desire to attain!

Did you know that at times what you need to do to improve your credit and finances may be difficult for your ears to hear and your eyes to see?

Even if you don't like hearing or seeing it <u>you must still address what needs to be addressed!</u>

Developing your mind to <u>where it needs to be financially</u> is no walk at the beach, however it is something that you must do if you desire to make your financial dreams come true!

Setting meaningful goals and taking the right actions consistently will get you to where you need to be in a much more efficient manner than if you fail to do so!

You must get to a point where you will not make excuses! You cannot do like 90% of the population <u>and make excuses or give reasons</u> and <u>never utilize their gift appropriately or attain their life purpose!</u>

Now is the time that you not only <u>obtain a breakthrough in your thinking</u>, but now is the time that you use that breakthrough to make great things happen in your life, not only for your benefit but your family's and future generations yet unborn!

Now is the time for a **mental re-awakening** where <u>you operate from the vantage point of success</u> in all that you do! Now is the time that <u>you take action</u> and do what will **lead to success** and not do what the other 90% do—which only leads to survival!

In this short read, you now have much of what you need to succeed and now is the time that you formulate your goals and take action without procrastination.

By doing so at this time you can reach your credit and financial destination and leave a legacy for the next generation!

Be sure to <u>put your goals in writing</u> and be sure to **A I M high** so that you can exceed the sky!

You must always realize that you can achieve **<u>any goal</u>** as long as you believe—and as long as you approach your future with the right **A** ttitude—**I** ntellect—and **M** otivation—or by having the right **A I M** on a consistent basis!

By <u>taking responsibility for your future</u> you will improve your **A I M** and you won't blame others <u>or forces that you feel are beyond your control.</u> Quite the contrary, you know that the power to do what needs to be done rests where it should be—inside of you!

You must always realize that you are bigger than any adversity that you have faced, are now facing or that you may face in your future!

You cannot let the adversity that you may face define you or destroy
your <u>determination</u> and <u>commitment level.</u>

Quite the contrary—<u>you must gain strength from the adversity that you will face</u> and move forward in a positive and inspiring manner and with a very high level of motivation.

By <u>setting meaningful goals</u> and having every intention on reaching those goals—<u>you will gain the strength that you need</u>—to succeed!

You will position your mind to gain the needed knowledge to move in the DIRECTION where SUCCESS lives, and it will be due in large part because you made the choice to **A I M** high at the right TIME!

In addition to having the right aim, you need to know how you manage your finances in the current economy as "effective money management" is a requirement today.

Do you have the money management personality and skills that are needed for success in today's economy?

Below are 5 of the more common personality types. If you have any of the following money management styles, there is no need to panic. You can resolve your credit and financial issues in your life regardless of where you are now at!

Do you have the money management skills that are needed for saving and investing long-term and are you willing to take control of your life currently?

If you don't make the decision to acquire the skills that are needed to manage your finances at a very high level, you are setting yourself up for potential problems later in your life.

By gaining a critical overview of the "money management personalities" you can position yourself and your family to utilize the best that is within you—to make your future dreams come true!

Learn About 5 Money Management Personalities **That Can Provide You Some Needed Insight on How You & Those Who You May Know Operate**

1) Strong Money Manager Personality

Some consumers seem to be natural savers and have a keen sense for wise money management.

They pay their credit card debt in a timely manner and rarely let the balance get to a high level. They normally have a consistent savings plan in place and have some real sense of their financial future.

2) Struggling Money Manager Personality

Other consumers seem to have difficulty saving, have high credit balances and struggle from paycheck to paycheck and they lack the ability to save in a meaningful way.

They have little concern for their financial future as they mainly live for the present or near present.

3) Decent Money Manager/Poor Credit User Personality

Still others can save effectively, yet they run up high credit card balances and have no real understanding of their financial future.

They may invest on a whim and in many cases <u>have no clue of what comprehensive financial planning is</u> and how it can help them attain their goals in the future in a more efficient manner

.

4) Non-believing Money Manager Personality

Others think they can't save, don't want to save, don't want to improve their finances <u>and they seem to be willing to take whatever life seems to dish out at them</u>—not looking for or expecting a better future.

When <u>"adversity"</u> occurs in their life they respond in an inappropriate manner. They often blame others or forces they feel are outside of their control for their current position in life!

5) Highly Informed Money Manager Personality

Still others have a sharp mind for their finances—can save at a high level, carry no credit card debt and seem to have their financial life in order.

Observations of Note on Money Management Personality Types:

With all of the above **money management personality types,** when pressed to explain their credit and financial approach in detail they all have varying answers—but none seem to hit the mark as far as having a true comprehensive understanding of what they need to do in their credit and financial life.

On many occasions even the high net worth and highly informed money manager had an inadequate emergency fund—due in large part to not properly understanding the "purpose" of an emergency fund!

In addition, many high net worth clients did not have an umbrella insurance policy that would have more appropriately protected them and their family from future financial risks.

Learn How You Can Improve Your Money Management Personality...

If you have a money management personality type like any of those mentioned above or a totally unique one—it is important that you realize the type of personality that you have!

All the **money management personality types** listed above have the potential to transform their credit and financial situation in an effective manner and manage their finances effectively over time.

The key is they receive and act on advice and information in a manner that <u>they understand</u> and <u>makes good financial sense to them.</u>

They can then <u>changed their way of looking at their situation</u> (have a different mindset) and start believing and knowing that <u>real credit and/or financial success</u> can happen for them and their family.

By willing to try something that was new, fresh and cutting edge and unlike any other system on the market, you may be able to find the solution to many of your concerns by looking within and seeing your situation for what it truly is. You can then began <u>implementing real steps</u> to address your concerns.

It is important that you realize that you can transform your money management personality if you are highly committed, and you sincerely want to do so.

Those who had an inappropriate money management personality lacked financial understanding in several key areas!

On many occasions when those who managed their finances poorly heard their favorite radio announcer, professional athlete or entertainer pitch a financial product they jumped on board in many cases.

However, in many of those cases they did not have <u>other key areas of their credit and finances addressed appropriately.</u>

They then invested in a stock or other commodity <u>with no real understanding</u> of how it would affect the other areas of their financial life.

Before you invest in a stock, mutual fund, gold, and other investments you must make sure that you have addressed your finances in an appropriate manner!

Don't do like many who invest in a haphazard manner—you must address all areas of your finances in a comprehensive manner and then you can position yourself to invest properly for the rest of your life.

Do not do like many and put the cart before the horse—by not understanding the right way to invest!

If you choose to invest without addressing all areas of your finances, you may be successful if your investment grows at the right rate. However, realize that it is a **dangerous strategy** even though it is often done successfully by many consumers.

If you decide to invest after you hear a convincing sales promotion that really impresses your heart and mind, and you truly feel that investment plan is for you, **you must stop—pause, and run through**

your mind—have I really addressed all of the key areas of my finances appropriately?

Furthermore, you must ask yourself, am I ready for the <u>responsibility that lies ahead</u> based on the <u>decision that I will make at this time?</u>

It is important that you realize that addressing all areas of your finances in a comprehensive manner and then investing is a wiser strategy if you want to achieve financial success at a high level on a consistent basis!

Final Thoughts on Money Management Personalities

Regardless of your **money management personality type** you must come to the realization that you can intelligently put a plan in place that can lead to a prosperous future for you and your family!

With the <u>right approach and the right systems in place</u> you can improve your and your family's credit and finances to a high level!

You can become the answer to your own concerns if you gain the preparation and knowledge that you need in a proactive manner.

If **you are sincere in your desire to achieve lasting success** and you accept your responsibility and you realize fully that you are accountable for your future success you can attain the future success that serves your best interest by taking the right actions in the right manner.

By doing so you can avoid the headaches that those who have a **money management personality** listed above that works against their best long-term interests have! You can gain the assurance "within your mind" that you can live your lifetime where you can leave **worry, anxiety, fear, frustration, lack of effort and excuses** behind you in the wind—exactly where they should be!

You must "always" remember that many who struggle financially do so because of a poor or non-existent **money management system.**

That poor or non-existent money management system is often the offspring **of having a poor or weak money management personality!**

The good news is that any "money management personality" **can be improved significantly by gaining the preparation and knowledge that is needed on a consistent basis!**

You must avoid the problems that we have seen many who mismanage their finances face over the years such as:

- spending more than they earn (you must plan and budget for success)

- not saving enough or not at all (you must have a consistent saving plan at some level)

- living at a level beyond their means (whether spending too much on housing, automobiles, clothing, social outings, and the list goes on and on)

- not appropriately saving for retirement (you must plan for your elderly years so that you can live abundantly), and

- lack of self-control (tapping into their retirement and other accounts when it is not in their best interest to do so)

You have the ability to improve upon your **money management personality** and transform your future into a more prosperous and productive one if you have the desire to make it happen at this time in an intelligent, consistent and proactive manner!

Be sure to **choose** success at a high level and not mediocrity in your credit and financial life as by doing so your **money management personality** and your future can take a turn for the better!

If you can see through it and you put your mind to it—you can do it! Isn't it time that you make something big happen in your life.

It often starts in a major way by properly selling your home and getting your finances in order at the earliest time possible!

We believe that **The FIZBO Manual** will provide you an avenue to success in the selling of your home and put you on a path to attaining many of your other goals and objectives that are yet unfulfilled in your life. You now know all of the key points that a **For Sale By Owner Seller (FIZBO)** needs to know if they sincerely desire to get results that will show!

Why abandon your dreams now when you could at this time decide to do something great for yourself and your family. Will you pursue financial gain, or will you continue to watch it rain?

It is important that you use the home selling tips, the goal setting bonus chapter and the money management techniques that you have learned in this concise guide to reach higher heights in your life.

You will be surprised at what a sincere effort toward creating an "action mindset" will produce in the selling of your home and the management of your finances throughout your life.

We wish you untold success in your and your family's future!

APPENDIX A

Thomas (TJ) Underwood—Real Estate Broker, Financial Planner, Author, Blogger

Thomas (TJ) Underwood is a real estate broker, former fee-only financial planner and loan officer who has served consumers in the Atlanta metropolitan area and throughout the world.

He has created over 700 pages of web-based content, created several books and e-books and continues to provide timely blog articles that have helped many around the world.

His inspiring, informative, entertaining, and highly beneficial articles have assisted visitors worldwide since 2010.

Thomas (TJ) Underwood blogs regularly at www.TheWealthIncreaser.com and offers real estate brokerage and financial planning services to paying clients at his Atlanta office.

If you are interested in having Thomas (TJ) Underwood prepare a debt payoff or comprehensive financial plan, please phone 404-952-9284 or email tj@TheWealthIncreaser.com to schedule an online consultation that will remain confidential.

You can also learn about other services that are offered by going to the following site:

https://www.thewealthincreaser.com/tfa-financial-planning/

If you desire to create a debt payoff or comprehensive financial plan yourself and would like a blueprint of how you can create your own, email tj@TheWealthIncreaser.com and put your debt payoff or comprehensive financial plan request in the subject box and he will respond to your request.

APPENDIX B

Thomas (TJ) Underwood/TFA Financial Planning

Thomas (TJ) Underwood has created over 700 pages of credit, finance, and wealth building articles covering the entire spectrum of personal finance on three websites.

The three sites have brought forth a new version of financial planning that turn the odds in your favor (not creditors) and more importantly puts you in control of your finances and wealth building activity in a way that could lead to greater success for you and your family throughout your lifetime.

With 2010 being the year of "when the blogging career of Thomas (TJ) Underwood all started" and 2020 (year of **1-2-3 Credit & Me** book being initially released) being the **ten-year anniversary** of blogging—**the author of 1-2-3 Credit & Me,** thought that it would be appropriate to provide **10** additional topics that could further lead to you achieving lasting success.

In the paragraphs below you will find **"10 success principles that came to mind as I was finalizing 1-2-3 Credit & Me"** that can help you achieve your financial (and life) goals at a higher level "in this and the coming decades" while you are here on planet earth. The following tips have been invaluable to many around the world and they are presented here in **The FIZBO Manual**, to help assist you so that you too can achieve at a higher level of excellence throughout your lifetime.

- **Know what to avoid**

It is important that you manage your finances from a standpoint of understanding <u>what</u> you need to avoid. You cannot let worry, anxiety, fear, frustration and lack of effort dominate your mental space.

By purchasing this book and frequenting www.TheWealthIncreaser.com and other wealth building sites you are showing a real commitment for successful outcomes to happen in your future.

- **Know what to confront**

In a similar manner as knowing what you must avoid in order to achieve optimally—you must also know what you need to confront. You must prepare your mind for success by gaining the right knowledge and using that knowledge appropriately.

You must not only have that knowledge—you must actually confront <u>your current cash flow position, your credit understanding and your financial understanding in all areas</u>—if you desire to achieve optimally throughout your lifetime.

- **Have a big imagination**

Nothing can hold you back more than your inability to dream big—and pursue those big dreams!

You must formulate significant goals and <u>have every intention within your mind</u> of achieving those goals.

- **Know your thought process**

How do you approach your finances and financial future? Do you even have an approach?

By <u>thinking about your future and what lies ahead</u> you put your heart and mind in position to receive the vibration and rhythms of life that can lead to <u>"life happenings"</u> going your way.

- **Begin with the end in mind**

You must begin with the end in mind whether it is a car purchase, home purchase, educational goals, retirement goals or any other goal.

By doing so you put yourself and your family in a more favorable position for success.

Will I sell or trade-in my vehicle in 3 years?

Will I stay in my home for 20 years and then move to my dream location?

Will I begin saving now to help fund my child's educational needs 15 years from now?

Will I allocate my risk profile with my investments in an appropriate manner? Will I sell stock X that I bought at $5 per share—all or in part—when it hits $20 a share?

Will I choose mutual funds, or will I use a stock portfolio to help reach the goals that I desire—or will I use a combination of investment vehicles to reach the goals that I desire?

Will I save appropriately so that I can reach my "retirement number" so that I can do what I desire in my retirement years?

The above—and **other probing questions** based on the goals that you are pursuing are what you must ask on the front end—so that you won't suffer on the back end!

- **Always know the importance of your credit score**

A good score generally starts at around 700 and the higher you go after that point the better.

You get into the great or excellent range once you score 750 or higher and that would put you in position to get the best rate in most transactions that involve credit.

Your mastery of the 5 credit factors that you have learned in this book has positioned you for the success that you desire at the various stages of your life as it relates to your credit and credit score.

- **Keep your monthly bills under 10 so that you can win**

You must make it a point to manage your bills monthly (mortgage, auto loan, gas, electric, water, garbage, phone, cable, and credit cards) at an optimal or highly effective level.

Keep in mind that if you are at nine bills or twelve bills you are still ok—the goal is 10 or so per month—to add clarity to your mind and thought process so that you reduce stress on a daily, monthly, and annual basis.

You must have <u>clarity</u> and <u>focus</u> on a daily basis and not allow clutter to cloud your mind!

By keeping the number of bills that you pay from your checking account on a monthly basis **under 10**—you set your living circumstances up <u>so that you can win.</u>

This success principle does not mean that you can't have other accounts to reach your <u>ultimate goals</u> such as an account for entertainment and living outside of your "fixed monthly expenses" or investment accounts and other accounts that are designed to help you reach your goals.

- **Know your money management personality**

By knowing how you manage your finances on a daily, weekly, monthly, and yearly basis—you put yourself far ahead of those in the general population who go about their daily activities in a manner where they don't have a clue.

Are you a <u>highly effective money manager</u>—or do you need to improve?

There is no need to panic as you can achieve lasting success regardless of your money management style.

- **Know where you are at in your life stage**

Whether you are just entering the work force, just graduating from college—or you have been working for years—it is important that you understand <u>the stage in life</u> that you are at.

By doing so <u>you add clarity to how you see your future</u> and you make reaching many of your goals more likely to occur.

- **Always establish a properly funded emergency fund**

It is imperative that you <u>establish an emergency fund</u> at the earliest time possible, and properly fund that emergency fund.

By doing so you help reduce the future risks that you will face in your life and success will be more likely to occur.

- **Have faith that what you are pursuing will truly occur**

You must know and act consistently in a manner that says to the universe—I will succeed!

You must **sincerely pursue the goals that you desire** so that you can give your mind added incentive—to reach higher!

You must **believe and know** that the results that you are pursuing—will show!

It is important that you use your **experience, expertise and you exercise the use of your mind in a spirit of excellence** if you desire to **achieve more** during your lifetime.

And just as "that process" led to the creation of three leading financial blogs, numerous books and e-books—and increased profitability for Realty 1 Strategic Advisors and TFA Financial Planning—so too can you use that process to make big things happen in your life.

Even though the **year of 2010** (my first year of blogging) started on an upbeat note with the creation of www.the-best-atlanta-real-estate-advice.com and later that year www.realty-1-strategic-advisors.com, the author of **The FIZBO Manual** would face great adversity in the spring of 2010 when the mentor of the creator of TheWealthIncreaser.com transitioned and even greater adversity later that same year when the younger brother who looks just like the author of **The FIZBO Manual** unexpectedly transitioned in the fall of 2010.

Those unfortunate events tested the faith of the author of **The FIZBO Manual,** however by responding positively to adversity in the same manner as I have urged you to do in this book—the continuous development of a number of sites took on a new meaning and increased urgency—and brought forth over 700 pages of web content that you can now benefit from <u>at this time</u> <u>along with the creation of a number of books in "The Real Estate & Finance 360 Degrees Series of Books" that are now on the market</u>.

Always realize that the success that you desire often begins by looking within and giving **<u>serious thought</u>** to what you desire most in your future. You must leave "all" <u>excuses or reasons why you can't reach your destiny</u> behind you, so that you can take the necessary steps toward making your dreams come true.

You must open your mind up to the inspiration <u>(and always be open to receiving inspiration when it is in your best interest to do so)</u> that will follow and you must have a strong desire on the inside of you—to make your dreams come true.

That <u>initial thought at a deep level</u> can lead you on a journey toward making the right moves <u>at the right time</u> and more effectively guide you toward your destiny!

In the end (or maybe the beginning depending on where you are now at) it is your timing, your willingness to move to action n, your preparation, your focus and an unstoppable belief on the inside of you—that will guide you in the direction of doing what you definitely need to do—to make your dreams come true.

Use what you were enshrined with at birth <u>(a spirit of excellence)</u> while you are here on planet earth!

It is of the opinion of the author of **The FIZBO Manual** that this book will act as a springboard to success and will help you achieve many of your financial goals.

However, you must realize that the opinion of the author of **The FIZBO Manual** is biased in favor of the author.

You must determine for yourself whether **The FIZBO Manual** is the best book for you—or whether there is another book on the market that will work better—as far as making your home selling dreams come true.

Always remember that the burning desire that you have on the inside at this time (or at some time in your future) to do "something big" may be the voice of God giving you the "ignition" that you need to help direct your steps and give you added strength to bring something new and powerful into this world—at a time and in a manner that is uniquely designed for you!

All the best to your continued success in the next ten years in your life—and beyond…

Currently **The Real Estate & Finance 360 Degrees Series of Books©** *consist of:*

Book 1) Managing & Improving Your Credit & Finances for this Millennium Paperback **Copyright© 2012**

Book 2) <u>HOME BUYER 411</u> *The Smart Guide to Buying Your Home*
E-book **Copyright© 2014, 2023** Hardback **Copyright© 2023**

Book 3) <u>HOME SELLER 411</u> *The Smart Guide to Selling Your Home*
E-book **Copyright© 2014,2023,** Hardback **Copyright© 2023**

Book 4) <u>The Wealth Increaser</u> E-book **Copyright© 2014,** Hardback **Copyright© 2023**

Book 5) The 3 Step Structured Approach to Managing Your Credit & Finances E-book **Copyright© 2014, 2023** Hardback **Copyright© 2023**

Book 6) The FIZBO Manual (**F**or **S**ale **B**y **O**wner Guide) E-book **Copyright© 2014, 2023** Hardback **Copyright© 2023**

Book 7) 1-2-3 Credit & Me E-book **Copyright© 2021, 2023** Paperback **Copyright© 2023,** Hardback **Copyright© 2023**

In addition, you can find helpful articles on several credit and finance topics by visiting the following websites:

www.the-best-atlanta-real-estate-advice.com

www.realty1sa.com

www.TheWealthIncreaser.com

I welcome your success stories and the positive effect that the books in the series along with the articles on the websites above have had on your life.

All the best…

Copyright© 2014, 2023

Publisher: TFA Financial Planning

Email: tj@TheWealthIncreaser.com

ISBN: 978-1-953994-10-3

- **Manage your home selling activities effectively throughout the process so that you can net the proceeds from sale in a realistic manner.**

- **Take charge of selling your home in a way that puts you in control and keeps you in control.**

- **Change your life in a major way by providing you a way to achieve major success in clear terms by providing you effective goal setting tips and ways to manage your money better prior to and after the selling of your home**

Thomas (TJ) Underwood is the Real Estate Broker at Realty 1 Strategic Advisors, LLC one of the most successful real estate and financial planning companies in the metropolitan Atlanta area. Realty 1 Strategic Advisors is based in Peachtree City, GA.

He is a former fee-only financial planner and top producing loan processor, and he has assisted clients from as far away as Germany with their real estate concerns. The concepts in **The FIZBO Manual** have been utilized by savvy home sellers to enhance the likelihood of a successful home sale and the achievement of many of their other goals during their lifetime.

He is also the creator of **TheWealthIncreaser.com**, one of the leading financial blog sites that can be found in the internet universe.

www.ingramcontent.com/pod-product-compliance
Lightning Source LLC
LaVergne TN
LVHW020935090426
835512LV00020B/3368